Democracy in USA
Biden call on Americans to take Seriously, the oncoming presidential election

By

Ronald R. Stein

Table of content:

Chapter 1.
Chapter 2.
Chapter 3.
Chapter 4.
Chapter 5.

Chapter 1.

Biden Call To All Americans

The president: My fellow Americans, please, if you have a seat, take it. I speak to you tonight from the sacred ground in America: Independence Hall in Philadelphia, Pennsylvania.

This is where America made its Declaration of Independence to the world more than two centuries ago with an idea, unique among nations, that in America, we're all created equal.

This is where the United States Constitution was written and debated.

This is where we set in motion the most extraordinary experiment of self-government the world has ever known with three simple words: "We, the People." "We, the People."

These two documents and the ideas they embody — equality and democracy — are the rock upon which this nation is built. They are how we became the greatest nation on Earth. They are why, for more than two centuries, America has been a beacon to the world.

But as I stand here tonight, equality and democracy are under assault. We do ourselves no favors to pretend otherwise.

So tonight, I have come to this spot where it all started to speak as honestly as I can to the country about the risks we face, about the power we have in our own hands to address these threats, and about the magnificent future that lies in front of us if only we choose it.

We must never forget: We, the people, are the genuine heirs of the American experiment that started more than two centuries ago.

We, the people, have burned within each of us the spark of liberty that was ignited here at Independence Hall – a light that illuminated our path through abolition, the Civil War, Suffrage, the Great Depression, world wars, and Civil Rights.

That holy spark still burns today in our time as we construct an America that is richer, freer, and fairer.

That is the task of my presidency, a mission I believe in with my entire soul.

But first, we must be honest with one another and with ourselves.

Too much of what's occurring in our nation now is not normal.

Donald Trump and the MAGA Republicans represent an extreme that challenges the fundamental basis of our nation.

Now, I want to be very clear — (applause) — very clear up front: Not every Republican, not even the majority of Republicans, are MAGA Republicans. Not every Republican adopts their extremist views.

I know because I've been able to deal with these mainstream Republicans.

But there is no doubt that the Republican Party today is controlled, pushed, and frightened by Donald Trump and the MAGA Republicans, and that is a menace to our nation.

These are hard things.

But I'm an American President – not the President of red America or blue America, but all America.

And I feel it is my obligation – my duty to level with you, to convey the truth no matter how tough, no matter how painful.

And here, in my judgment, is what is true: MAGA Republicans do not respect the Constitution. They do not believe in the rule of law. They do not acknowledge the will of the people.

They refuse to accept the results of a free election. And they're trying right now, as I speak, in state after state to hand authority to determine elections in America to partisans and cronies, allowing election doubters to destroy democracy itself.

MAGA forces are determined to move our nation backward – backward to an America where there is no freedom to choose, no right to privacy, no access to contraception, and no right to marry who you love.

They encourage authoritarian leaders, and they feed the fires of political violence that are a danger to our liberties, to the pursuit of justice, to the rule of law, to the very essence of this nation.

They look at the crowd who invaded the United States Capitol on January 6th — viciously assaulting law officers — not as insurrectionists who stuck a knife to the neck of our democracy, but they look at them as patriots.

And they consider their MAGA failure to halt a peaceful transition of power after the 2020 election as preparation for the 2022 and 2024 elections.

They attempted everything last time to negate the votes of 81 million people. This time, they're determined to succeed in blocking the will of the people.

That's why reputable conservatives, like Federal Circuit Court Judge Michael Luttig, have dubbed Trump and the hardline MAGA Republicans, quote, a "clear and present danger" to our democracy.

But although the danger to American democracy is genuine, I want to state as loudly as we can: We are not helpless in the face of these attacks.
We are not spectators in this continuous onslaught on democracy.

There are much more Americans — far more Americans from every — from every background and creed that reject the extreme MAGA philosophy than those who support it. (Applause.)

And, friends, it is within our ability, it's in our hands — yours and mine — to halt the attack on American democracy.

I think America is at an inflection point — one of those moments that decide the form of everything that's to come after.

And now America must choose: to go ahead or to regress backward? To develop the future or worry about the past? To be a country of hope and togetherness and optimism, or a nation of fear, division, and of darkness?

MAGA Republicans have made their pick. They welcome rage. They thrive on turmoil. They live not in the light of truth but the darkness of falsehoods.

But we — collectively, we can choose a new route. We can select a better way. Forward to the future. A future of potential. A future to develop and dream and hope.

And we're on that route, going forward.
I know this country. I know you, the American people. I know your bravery. I know your hearts. And I know our history.
This is a country that cherishes our Constitution. We do not reject it. (Applause.)

This is a country that believes in the rule of law. We do not disavow it. (Applause.)

This is a country that appreciates free and fair elections. We respect the will of the people. We do not deny it. (Applause.)

And this is a country that opposes violence as a political tactic. We do not advocate violence.

We are still an America that believes in honesty and decency and respect for others, patriotism, liberty, justice for everyone, hope, and possibilities.

We are still, at our essence, a democracy. (Applause.)

And yet history teaches us that mindless allegiance to a single leader and a readiness to participate in political violence is toxic to democracy.

For a long time, we've convinced ourselves that American democracy is assured, but it's not.

We have to defend it, protect it, and stand up for it — every One of us.

That's why today I'm urging our country to join together, and unify behind the one cause of safeguarding our democracy regardless of your philosophy. (Applause.)

We're all obligated, by duty and morality, to resist fanatics who would put their desire for power above everything else.

Democrats, independents, mainstream Republicans: We must be stronger, more resolute, and more devoted to protecting American democracy than MAGA Republicans are to — to destroying American democracy.

We, the people, will not allow anybody or anything to pull us apart. Today, there are threats surrounding us we cannot let to triumph. We hear — you've heard it — more and more discussion of violence as an acceptable political instrument in our nation. It's not. It can never be an acceptable instrument.

So I want to say something straight and simple: There is no place for political violence in America. Period. None. Ever. (Applause.)

We watched police enforcement violently assault us on January 6th. We've seen election officials, and poll workers — many of them volunteers of both parties — exposed to intimidation and death threats.

And — can you believe it? — FBI officers merely performing their job as ordered, facing threats to their own lives from their own fellow Americans.

On top of that, there are prominent personalities — today, yesterday, and the day before – anticipating and all but advocating for widespread bloodshed and rioting in the streets.

This is inflammatory. It's risky. It's against the rule of law. And we, the people, must say: This is not who we are. (Applause.)

Ladies and gentlemen, we can't be pro-ex- — pro-insurrectionist and pro-American. They're incompatible. (Applause.)

We can't allow violence to be normalized in our nation. It's wrong. We individually have to reject political violence — with all the moral clarity and conviction our country can summon. Now.

We can't allow the integrity of our elections to be damaged, because it is a route to anarchy.

Look, I know poli- — politics can be ferocious and cruel and terrible in America. I got it. I believe in the give-and-take of politics, in disagreement and discussion and dissent.

We're a large, multifaceted nation. But democracy thrives only if we, the people, maintain the guardrails of the republic. Only if we, the people, accept the results of free and fair elections. (Applause.) Only if we, the people, regard politics not as complete conflict but as mediation of our disagreements.

Democracy cannot endure when one side feels there are only two options to an election: either they win or they were tricked.
And that's where MAGA Republicans are now. (Applause.)

They don't comprehend what every patriotic American knows: You can't love your nation just when you win. (Applause.) It's essential.

American democracy only works if we choose to respect the rule of law and the institutions that were established up in this chamber behind me, only if we respect our genuine political disagreements.

I will not stand by and watch — I will not — the will of the American people be reversed by crazy conspiracy theories and unfounded, evidence-free charges of fraud.

I will not stand by and see elections in our nation stolen by individuals who just refuse to acknowledge that they lost. (Applause.)

I will not stand by and let the most basic right in our nation — the ability to vote and have your vote counted — and — be stripped from you and the American people. (Applause.)

Look, as your President, I will defend our democracy with every fiber of my being, and I'm asking every American to join me. (Applause.)
(A protester's disruption can be heard.)

Throughout our history, America has frequently achieved the greatest progress coming out of some of our darkest periods, as you're hearing in that bullhorn.
I think we can and we must do it again, and we are.

MAGA Republicans look at America and see destruction and misery and despair. They propagate fear and deception –- lies uttered for profit and power.

But I envision a different America — an America with infinite potential, an America that is set to take off. I hope you see it as well. Just look around.

I felt we could pull America from the depths of COVID, so we approved the greatest economic recovery package since Franklin Delano Roosevelt. And now, America's economy is quicker and stronger than any other advanced country in the globe. (Applause.) We have more to go.

I felt we could create a better America, so we approved the greatest infrastructure investment since President Dwight D. Eisenhower. And we've now launched a decade of rebuilding\The nation's roads, bridges, highways, ports, water systems, high-speed Internet, and trains. (Applause.)

I felt we could make America safer, so we enacted the most major gun safety bill since President Clinton. (Applause.)

I felt we could move from having the highest cost of medications in the world to making prescription drugs and healthcare more reasonable, so we approved the most important healthcare changes since President Obama signed the Affordable Care Act. (Applause.)

And I believed we could create — we could create a clean energy future and save the planet, so we passed the most important climate initiative ever, ever, ever. (Applause.)

The cynics and the critics tell us nothing can get done, but they are wrong. There is not a single thing America cannot do — not a single thing beyond our capacity if we do it together.

It's never easy. But we're demonstrating that in America, no matter how long the path, progress does come. (Applause.)

Look, I know the last year — a few years have been tough. But today, COVID no longer controls our lives. More Americans are working than ever.
 Businesses are increasing. Our schools are open. Millions of Americans have been pulled out of poverty. Millions of soldiers who were exposed to hazardous burn pits will finally receive what they deserve for their families and the company- — recompense. (Applause.)

American manufacturing has come alive throughout the Heartland, and the future will be produced in America — (applause) — no matter what the white supremacists and the fanatics say.

I put a bet on you, the American people, and that investment is paying off. Proving that from darkness – the darkness of Charlottesville, of COVID, of gun violence, of revolt — we can see the light. Light is becoming apparent. (Applause.)

The light that will guide us forward not only in words but in actions — actions for you, for your children, for your grandchildren, for America.

Even at this moment, with all the challenges we face, I give you my word as a Biden: I've never been more optimistic about America's future. Not because of me, but because of who you are.

We're going to eliminate cancer as we know it. Mark my words. (Applause.)

We are going to generate millions of new employment in a clean energy economy.

We're going to think big. We're going to make the 21st century another American century because the world needs us to. (Applause.)

That's where we need to focus our energy — not on the past, not on divisive culture wars, not on the politics of grievance, but on a future we can build together.

The MAGA Republicans believe that for them to succeed, everyone else has to fail. They believe in America — not as I believe about America.

I think America is large enough for all of us to prosper, and that is the country we're building: a society where no one is left behind.

I ran for President because I thought we were in a struggle for the soul of this country. I still think that to be true. I think the soul is the breath, the vitality, and the essence of who we are. The soul is what makes us "us."

The essence of America is characterized by the holy concept that all are created equal in the image of God. That all are entitled to be treated with decency, dignity, and respect. Those all deserve fairness and a chance at lives of wealth and significance. And that democracy — democracy must be preserved because democracy makes all these things possible. (Applause.) Folks, it's up to us.

Democracy originates and will be sustained in us, the people's habits of heart, in our character: optimism that is tested\syet persists, bravery that digs deep when we need it, empathy that drives democracy, the desire to view each other not as adversaries but as fellow Americans.

Look, our democracy is faulty. It always has been.

Notwithstanding the guys, you hear on the other side there. They're allowed to be obnoxious. This is a democracy. But history and common sense — (applause) — good manners is nothing they've ever suffered from.

But history and common sense tell us that opportunity, liberty, and justice for everyone are most likely to come to fruition in a democracy.

We have never completely achieved the ambitions of our founding, but every generation has opened those doors a little wider to welcome more individuals who have been excluded previously.

My fellow Americans, America is a concept — the most powerful notion in the history of the planet. And it beats in the hearts of the people of this country.

It beats in all of our hearts. It unifies America. It is the American creed.

The idea is that America guarantees that everyone is treated with dignity. It gives hate no safe harbor. It puts in everyone the notion that no matter where you start in life, there's nothing you can't accomplish.

That's who we are. That's what we stand for. That's what we believe. And that is exactly what we are doing: opening doors, generating new opportunities, and concentrating on the future. And we're just begun. (Applause.)

Our goal is to make our country free and fair, just and powerful, noble and full.

And this job is the labor of democracy – the work of this generation. It is the work of our time, for all time.
We can't afford to have — leave anybody on the sidelines. We need everyone to do their

part. So speak out. Speak out. Get engaged. Vote, vote, vote. (Applause.)

And if we all do our part — if we do our duty in 2022 and beyond, then centuries yet to come will say we — all of us here — we maintained the faith. We maintained democracy. (Applause.) We heeded our war — we — we obeyed not our darkest inclinations but our better angels. And we demonstrated that, with all its shortcomings, America is still the light to the world, an ideal to be fulfilled, a promise to be maintained.

There is nothing more important, nothing more sacred, nothing more American. That's our soul. That's who we genuinely are. And that's who must — we must always be.
And I have no doubt — none –– that this is who we will be and that we'll come together as a nation. That we'll protect our democracy. That for the next 200 years,

we'll have what we had the last 200 years: the greatest country on the face of the Earth.

We simply need to remember who we are. We are the United States of America. The United States of America.

<u>Chapter 2.</u>

The United States is at a dangerous junction in its battle to maintain democracy, President Joe Biden believes

(America Democracy As Never Known Before)

"There's no question that the Republican Party today is dominated, driven, and intimidated by Donald Trump and the MAGA Republicans," Biden said, referring to Trump's 2016 campaign slogan, Make America Great Again. "And that is a threat to this country."

Biden drew a dark picture of his opponents' vision for America as he spoke in front of the hall where the nation's founders wrote and debated both the Declaration of Independence and the U.S. Constitution, nearly 250 years ago.

He spoke for 25 minutes, and in that time, said one word no fewer than 25 times: democracy.

He used the word as a cudgel against Trump-aligned Republicans who echo Trump's claim that the 2020 election was stolen; who work to suppress voter turnout in key states; and who participated in the violent insurrection attempt at the U.S. Capitol on Jan. 6, 2021.

"History tells us that blind loyalty to a single leader and a willingness to engage in political violence is fatal to democracy," he said "For a long time, we've told ourselves that American democracy is guaranteed. But it's not. We have to defend it. Protect it. Stand up for it."

In a refutation delivered ahead of the speech, House Republican leader Kevin McCarthy accused Biden of divisiveness and blamed Democrats for rising inflation, crime, and government spending.

"In the past two years, Joe Biden has launched an assault on the soul of America, on its people, on its laws, on its most sacred values," he said. "He has launched an assault on our democracy. His policies have severely wounded America's soul, diminished America's spirit, and betrayed America's trust."

Biden's condemnation earned him hecklers, who shouted obscenities in his direction as he spoke. Going momentarily off-script, he responded.

"Those folks over there, they're entitled to be outrageous," he said. "This is a democracy."

US President Joe Biden arrives with first lady Jill Biden to speak outside Independence Hall, on Sept. 1, 2022, in Philadelphia.
US President Joe Biden arrives with first lady Jill Biden to speak outside Independence Hall, on Sept. 1, 2022, in Philadelphia.

But he also used the word to reflect what he believes is a better future, led by his party, whose recent legislative gains he touted as proof. Since taking office, Biden has shepherded through major legislation that his administration says will bring about economic recovery, massive infrastructure improvements, gun safety, affordable health care, clean energy, and climate change reduction.

"Together, together, we can choose a different path," he said. "We can choose a better path forward to the future. A future of possibility, a future to build a dream and hope – and we're on that path moving ahead."

This is Biden's second visit to the Keystone State this week. Pennsylvania is a competitive state in what is shaping up as a battleground between Biden's Democrats and Trump's Republicans in midterm elections later this year.

Earlier in the day, White House press secretary Karine Jean-Pierre stressed that this was not intended as a stump speech.
There's no question that the Republican Party today is dominated, driven, and intimidated by Donald Trump and the MAGA Republicans," Biden said, referring to Trump's 2016 campaign slogan, Make America Great Again. "And that is a threat to this country."

Biden drew a dark picture of his opponents' vision for America as he spoke in front of the hall where the nation's founders wrote and debated both the Declaration of Independence and the U.S. Constitution, nearly 250 years ago.

He spoke for 25 minutes, and in that time, said one word no fewer than 25 times: democracy.

He used the word as a cudgel against Trump-aligned Republicans who echo Trump's claim that the 2020 election was stolen; who work to suppress voter turnout in key states; and who participated in the violent insurrection attempt at the U.S. Capitol on Jan. 6, 2021.

"History tells us that blind loyalty to a single leader and a willingness to engage in political violence is fatal to democracy," he said "For a long time, we've told ourselves that American democracy is guaranteed. But it's not. We have to defend it. Protect it. Stand up for it."

In a refutation delivered ahead of the speech, House Republican leader Kevin McCarthy accused Biden of divisiveness and blamed Democrats for rising inflation, crime, and government spending.

"In the past two years, Joe Biden has launched an assault on the soul of America, on its people, on its laws, on its most sacred values," he said. "He has launched an assault on our democracy. His policies have severely wounded America's soul, diminished America's spirit, and betrayed America's trust."

Biden's condemnation earned him hecklers, who shouted obscenities in his direction as he spoke. Going momentarily off-script, he responded.

"Those folks over there, they're entitled to be outrageous," he said. "This is a democracy."

But he also used the word to reflect what he believes is a better future, led by his party, whose recent legislative gains he touted as proof.

Since taking office, Biden has shepherded through major legislation that his administration says will bring about economic recovery, massive infrastructure improvements, gun safety, affordable health care, clean energy, and climate change reduction.

"This is so much broader, so much bigger than any one party, than any one person," she said. "And it's an optimistic speech, again, about where we are as a nation and where we can go.

And it's about the fundamental struggle around the globe between autocracy and democracy and how democracy is a critical foundation for this country to move forward."

Analysts question that, as Biden's recent legislative victories and priorities don't overlap much with the themes of his speech.

"We're beginning to see what issues that Democrats see as being advantageous: guns are one, democracy is another," said William Howell, a professor of American politics at the University of Chicago. "And it's interesting, too, that he didn't do much legislatively on either of those domains. And yet those are the ones he's talking about, but to pass policy now but to reshape the composition of Congress."

Historians who study presidential rhetoric say Biden's tone has shifted noticeably as the November polls have gotten closer.

"I believe the sharper rhetoric from the president and other Democrats is working," said Jeremi Suri, a history professor at the University of Texas at Austin. "There's evidence that many independent voters – not Trump voters, many independent voters – particularly women, even in conservative states, like Texas and Kansas, are fed up with Republican obstructionism. And quite frankly, they're fed up with the news of law-breaking by the former president. The more Trump is in the news, the better the Democrats look."

After the speech, Suri noted that Biden's words may now put his opponents on a back foot.

"Biden's speech forces Republicans like [Senate Minority Leader Mitch] McConnell and McCarthy to either defend or renounce MAGA Republicans — no way to avoid the issue when commenting on this speech," he said.

But on this night in Philadelphia — as the president urged Americans to "vote, vote,

vote" — he closed with a picture of the country he saw

"We are the United States of America, the United States of America," he said, stressing the word "united." "And may God protect our nation. And may God protect all those who stand watch over our democracy. God bless you all. Democracy. Thank you."

Biden warns the U.S. faces a powerful threat from anti-democratic forces
Biden, in a prime-time address, says Trump and "MAGA Republicans" are mounting a dangerous attack on the country's values, and Americans must fight back

Biden denounces 'MAGA Republicans,' urges optimism
In a fiery speech, President Biden explained how extremist Republicans are threatening American democracy.

PHILADELPHIA — President Biden delivered a forceful address Thursday on what he called a dangerous assault on American democracy, warning that "too much of what's happening in our country today is not normal" as "Donald Trump and the MAGA Republicans represent an extremism that threatens the very foundations of our republic."

Biden's speech, outside Philadelphia's Independence Hall, was a remarkable assessment from a sitting president that the fabric of American governance is under serious threat — "we do ourselves no favors to pretend otherwise," he said. While Biden did not name Republicans other than the former president, he warned of election deniers who have won Republican primaries and those who have sought to overturn legitimate elections.

"We are still at our core a democracy — yet history tells us that blind loyalty to a single leader, and the willingness to engage in political violence, is fatal to democracy," Biden said. "There is no question that the Republican Party is dominated, driven, and intimidated by Donald Trump and the MAGA Republicans."

Biden on Thursday appeared to seek a balance between the lofty tones of a presidential address and the sharp, personal criticism of Republicans that many in his party believe is necessary to meet a moment of crisis. While paying tribute to the country's grand historical traditions, Biden also suggested the upcoming election is a battle between those embracing American values and those trying to destroy them.

White House officials stressed repeatedly that Biden's speech was not political, saying the defense of democracy is hardly a partisan topic. While Biden did criticize Republicans, he made it clear he was only attacking what he called "MAGA

Republicans," a reference to those who are loyal to Trump and his false claims of rigged elections.

The speech unfolded at a moment of remarkable turmoil in American politics. The Justice Department is investigating whether Trump improperly took hundreds of classified documents to his home in Florida and whether his employees obstructed efforts to get them back.

As Trump weighs another White House run — while falsely claiming he won in 2020 — a House committee has disclosed vivid details of his role in the Jan. 6, 2021, assault on the U.S. Capitol. Meanwhile, Republicans have been nominating an array of candidates for office who falsely claim the 2020 vote was rigged and appear ready to rewrite election rules in their states.

Biden spoke before the majestic backdrop of Independence Hall, colored by red and blue spotlights, where the Declaration of Independence and Constitution were shaped. Uniformed Marines stood on each side of the hall's main door and large American flags were unfurled behind the president.

Biden sought to frame the current moment as one of the tests that have periodically arisen in American history. It is "one of those moments that determines the shape of everything that comes after, and now America must choose to move forward or to move backward," Biden said. "This is a nation that believes in the rule of law. We do not repudiate it. This is a nation that respects free and fair elections. We honor the will of the people, we do not deny it."

Many Democrats and activists have long complained that Biden was doing too little and speaking too mildly, to take on the threat from a pro-Trump movement that is seeking to undermine past and future elections, and Thursday's speech was one of his most forceful since taking office. Biden can often stumble over his words or abandon a sentence in midstream, but on Thursday he appeared focused and energized.

The speech was delivered outdoors, and Biden was repeatedly heckled by protesters yelling "Let's go, Brandon" and the more vulgar version of that slogan. Biden periodically referred to the hecklers, at one point saying: "They're entitled to be outrageous. This is a democracy."

House Minority Leader Kevin McCarthy (R-Calif.), in remarks ahead of the speech, portrayed the president as a divisive figure who dismisses much of the country, saying Biden should apologize "for slandering tens of millions of Americans as 'fascists.' " At a fundraiser last week, Biden accused many in the Republican Party of moving toward "semi-fascism."

Referring to Biden's oft-repeated line about restoring the soul of America, McCarthy said, "What Joe Biden doesn't understand is that the soul of America is in the tens of millions of hard-working people, of loving families of law-abiding citizens, [whom he] vilified for simply wanting a strong, safer and more prosperous country."

Some Republicans, including those who have repudiated Trump, criticized Biden's speech as divisive.

"I don't hate Biden's thesis, but that speech was so full of divisive language that goes well beyond the 'MAGA base.' A step backward for Biden on a critically important topic," Alyssa Farah Griffin, a former Trump official who has since criticized the former president and his political movement,
Biden said Thursday that he was not taking issue with those who disagree with him or come from another political party, but

rather with those who challenge the principles the country was founded on.

"I believe I have to level with you, to tell the truth, no matter how difficult, no matter how painful," Biden said. "And here in my view is what is true: MAGA Republicans do not respect the Constitution. They do not believe in the rule of law. They do not recognize the will of the people. They refuse to accept the results of a free election."

He added, "They promote authoritarian leaders and they fan the flames of political violence that are a threat to our rights, to our pursuit of justice, to the rule of the law, to the very soul of this country."

This was Biden's second visit this week to the swing state of Pennsylvania, with a third scheduled for Monday. Biden did not mention him, but the Republican candidate for governor of Pennsylvania, Doug Mastriano, has promoted Trump's claim of a stolen election and promised, if elected, to overhaul the state's long-standing election procedures. Democrats are also seeking to win a critical Senate seat in the state in hopes of maintaining control of the chamber.

Despite his dire warnings, the president also sought to strike a note of optimism, saying that far more people "reject the extreme MAGA ideology than those who accept it."

"While the threat to American democracy is real, I want to say as clearly as we can: We are not powerless in the face of these threats. We are not bystanders to this ongoing attack on democracy," Biden said. "It's in our power. It's in our hands — yours and mine — to stop the assault on American democracy."
The president urged Americans to focus on the future, rather than litigate the past or expend energy on "divisive culture wars" or "politics of grievance."

Biden also repeatedly condemned the use of violence as a tool to intimidate political opponents, citing election workers, poll workers, and FBI agents who have endured threats, in part due to Trump's rhetoric. That rhetoric has escalated in recent days as the former president engages in a hard-fought legal battle over the FBI's recovery of classified documents that Trump brought to his home in Florida.

"There are dangers around us we cannot allow to prevail," Biden said. "We hear more and more talk about violence as an acceptable political tool in this country. It is not. It can never be an acceptable political tool."

Biden also referred indirectly, as he has before, to recent comments from Sen. Lindsey O. Graham (R-S.C.) predicting that there will be "riots in the street" if Trump is criminally charged for taking the documents or obstructing justice.

Polls show that a majority of Americans are concerned about the state of democracy — an unusual development, given that issues like the economy usually dominate voters' concerns. Worries about democracy have become a top voter issue for November's midterms as Trump continues to falsely insist the 2020 election was stolen and as some Republican candidates embrace that position.

A Quinnipiac University poll released this week found that by a 67 to 29 percent margin, Americans think the nation's democracy is in danger of collapse — a nine-point increase from January when it was 58 to 37 percent.

And a CNN poll in June/July of this year found that 58 percent of Americans were "just a little" or "not at all" confident that elections in America reflect the will of the people. That was up sharply from January 2021, when 40 percent doubted that elections reflected the will of the public.

The views of the source of the threat to America's democracy vary sharply between the parties. Republicans are more likely to believe that elections are fraudulent or rigged by their opponents, while Democrats fear that the GOP is moving to suppress votes and change the rules in their favor.
In the most recent CNN poll, 71 percent of Republicans, 62 percent of independents, and 43 percent of Democrats said they lacked confidence that election results in the United States reflect the will of the people.

For much of his presidency, Biden has sought to avoid directly attacking Trump or citing individual Republicans by name for their embrace of anti-democratic positions.

But that has changed in recent weeks as he has more directly attacked "MAGA Republicans" who he argues pose an existential threat to the nation's future.

During a political rally last week, Biden said many of them "embrace political violence."
At Constitution Hall, Biden said he was not maligning all Republicans or those who disagreed with him, but rather what he called extremist forces that have undermined election results and stoked political violence.

He understands that politics can be nasty, he said, but the United States is a "big, complicated country" that could only endure if people accepted election results, whether their candidate wins or not.

"Democracy cannot survive when one side believes there are only two outcomes to an election — either they win or they were cheated. And that's where the MAGA Republicans are today," Biden said.

"They don't understand what every patriotic American knows: You can't love your country only when you win."

"I will not stand by and watch elections in this country stolen by people who simply refuse to accept that they lost," Biden said. "I will not stand by and watch the most fundamental freedom in this country — the freedom to vote and having your vote counted — taken from the American people."

Chapter 3.

Key point to acknowledge from Joe Biden's warning on the Republican threat to Democracy.

President Biden told the public that American democracy is under attack by his biggest political opponent.

"Donald Trump and the MAGA Republicans represent an extreme that threatens the very basis of our republic," he declared from the site of the birth of American democracy, the signing of the Declaration of Independence in Philadelphia.

1. This speech did not shy away from politics.

Biden isn't aiming to come out as political when he speaks about democracy, a senior White House official told reporters earlier in the day — and he would not attempt to convince the people to vote for his party.

And no matter what the president said today, it was almost unavoidable that this address would be perceived as political. Republican candidates considerably more commonly reject election outcomes than Democrats.

Biden has been out in front of his party in talking about this, using strong rhetoric that made even some Democrats quiver. "It's like semi-fascism," he declared on the campaign trail lately, citing the attitude he claims underlying the extreme side of the Republican Party.

That has provided Republicans an occasion to portray him as overreaching with his concerns about the status of democracy.

Right before the president's speech, House Minority Leader Kevin McCarthy (R-Calif.) said Biden should first apologize to Trump supporters "for slandering tens of millions of Americans as 'fascists.'"

Instead of shying away from that type of rhetoric, Biden named his probable 2024 opponent by name.

Though the president did take care to say there are "mainstream Republicans" who do not subscribe to an "extreme ideology" — a line that drew applause — he also continued: "There's no question that the Republican Party today is dominated, driven and intimidated by Donald Trump and the MAGA Republicans."

He went on to relate what he dubbed "MAGA Republicans" to numerous GOP state legislatures' controversial abortion laws, as well as to the most conservative Supreme Court judge, Clarence Thomas, who intimated in his recent abortion judgment that the court may take back same-sex marriage rights.

"MAGA Republicans want to drag America backward, backward to an America where there is no freedom to choose, no right to privacy, no access to contraception, no right to marry who you love," Biden stated.

Other sections of the speech emphasized a pro-Democrat (and not just generically pro-democracy) message: Toward the conclusion of his talk, Biden again championed his recent legislative achievements.

Then there's the timing: This speech comes just two months before consequential midterm elections for his party, and just days before he'll kick off campaigning for Democrats in the midterms, including in Wisconsin and Pennsylvania over Labor Day.

Biden also faced considerable criticism for putting Marines behind him when he delivered this address.

2. There isn't much Democrats can do about the concerns Biden mentioned – for now, "It is within our power.
It's in our hands, yours and mine, to halt the attack on American democracy," Biden addressed the country, But for a year, Democrats failed to enact national voting rights legislation that would have overcome voting limitations in Republican-led states.

Biden — as he does with so many topics that Congress fails to solve — sought to act on his own through executive measures.

But they were rather small, including instructing the heads of government departments to identify methods to boost voter registration and information on how to seek votes. The Justice Department also sued Georgia over its restricted voting statute, charging the state with racial discrimination; primaries this summer went place with the new restrictions still in force.

Democrats had the votes for establishing federal voting standards, given that Sens. Joe Manchin III (D-W.Va.) and Kyrsten Sinema (D-Ariz.) never opposed making federal reforms to voting rules (but the devil was in the details) (although the devil was in the details). But the two senators rejected overcoming the filibuster and approving this despite Republican opposition.

That may change if Democrats have a spectacular midterm election: The Washington Post's Paul Kane wisely observes that because of underperforming Republican candidates, Senate Democrats might win elections in November in as many as six states. It's a lofty order, considering elections traditionally go poorly for the party that occupies the White House, but it's conceivable — and winning all six would mean they would add to their majority, holding up to 52 seats instead of the 50 they have now. That would mean they wouldn't need Manchin or Sinema for every piece of legislation they want to pass that doesn't have any Republican support.

Biden has spoken about this on the campaign trail: "If we elect two more senators, [if] we hold the House ... we're going to get a lot of unfinished work done."

3. Democracy has become a driving force on the left.
A few months before the election, "threats to democracy" is now the top voter worry, above even "cost of living" and "jobs and the economy," according to an August NBC survey.

Interestingly, this topic is gaining so much attention, especially on the left.

(When it comes to democracy, topics like campaign funding and selecting judges have generally energized the right.) That political situation began to alter following the 2020 election and in 2021, when Democrats launched their huge, ultimately unsuccessful, effort to gain nationwide voting rights.

As Michael Waldman, president of the Brennan Center for Justice, told me in an interview at the time: "Now the 'big lie' has become a mobilizing and motivating issue on the right in the way it never was before, and for the first time, the push for stronger democracy protections have become a central motivating issue for progressives and Democrats."

4. *Biden aimed at the many Republicans who thought Jan. 6 was a valid protest.*

Early on in his address, he attempted to separate "MAGA Republicans" from the rest of the Republican Party, stating not all Republicans had anti-democratic impulses.

He's right: there are major, serious cracks splitting Republicans along those lines. But there is plenty of evidence that this combination controls the party.

Take the Jan. 6, 2021, assault on the Capitol. On Thursday night, Biden urged all Americans to denounce what transpired as abhorrent political violence.

Yet in a survey done last summer by Monmouth University, more Republicans termed Jan. 6 a "legitimate protest" rather than even a "riot," as The Post's Aaron Blake pointed out. According to that study, only 13 percent of Republicans thought Jan. 6 constituted an uprising.

If Republicans win back control of the House in November's midterm elections, they are likely to marginalize or possibly abolish the congressional Jan.

6 committees investigating the attack. And as Trump prepares to start his presidential candidacy, he declared Thursday that if elected, he'll award pardons to Jan. 6 defendants accused of engaging in the attack.

"We can't be pro-insurrectionist and pro-American. They're incompatible," Biden stated Thursday.

Yet a recent survey reveals that a majority of major party in America don't view it that way.

<u>*Chapter 4.*</u>

How 'alternative facts' imperil US democracy.

As disparities in society develop, a vision of a common reality is eroding, social scientists warn.

(About the previous incident) The Truth Illusion picture, On a fresh, bright day in Maryland, United States, in March 2021, President Joe Biden stepped onto the red carpet-lined steps of Air Force One. Four seconds after he started ascending to the aircraft's entry, he slid.

He reached down, balanced himself on one of the steps with his left hand, and started ascending again. He stumbled a second time. Two steps later, he fell again - this time falling awkwardly on his left leg. He rose, gripping the guide rail, dusted down his suit pants, and went once again – more carefully this time – towards the plane's entrance.

The White House press office promptly produced a statement declaring the president was "100 percent fine" and that he'd been pushed off balance by a gust of wind. But the occurrence, just 58 days into his presidency, was grabbed upon by Biden's opponents as evidence that the 78-year-old leader was simply not physically robust enough to carry out his job.

After a vicious 2020 presidential campaign, it is not unexpected that videos of Biden stumbling frequently would garner harsh remarks from Republicans who lost to Biden.

After all, similar concerns over fitness for office were raised by Democrats just eight months earlier when then-President Donald Trump was seen walking unsteadily down a ramp at West Point Military Academy in

New York (Trump, who had turned 74 the day before he visited West Point, later claimed that his "leather-bottomed shoes" made it difficult for him to manage the "slippery" walk).

Differing assessments of the two leader's physical ability can be dismissed as petty political sniping, but responses inside the US to these two occasions hint at possibly one of the most complex questions confronting America today: What is the truth?

Was Biden swept off his feet by the wind, or did he stumble? Were the soles of Trump's shoes genuinely to blame for the way he walked at West Point, or was there another reason? Have physical slip-ups by the two males been re-versioned by those who seek to obfuscate the facts of what truly took place?

<u>*Chapter 5.*</u>

This is where I will be sharing with you some insights into disagreements on a shared reality that have caused increasing – and deeper – divisions across the US.

Where once-respected professionals — teachers, scientists, journalists, politicians, and others – are today accused of manipulating facts to achieve their extremist agendas.

That proclivity to falsify facts was made painfully obvious by Donald Trump's lawyer, former New York City Mayor Rudy Giuliani, in a televised interview with NBC's Chuck Todd on the Meet the Press program in August 2018.

"Truth isn't truth," Giuliani stated.

Qassim Cassam is a professor of philosophy from Warwick University in the United

Kingdom who focuses on self-knowledge, Kantian epistemology, and perception. He likens the statement to the moment in George Orwell's classic, 1984, in which the character Winston Smith is being tortured by a representative of Big Brother to induce him to believe that two plus two equals five.

"And Winston has terrible problems grasping that two plus two equals five," Cassam continues. "And he has a huge problem accepting that for the simple reason that two plus two is not five."

Indeed, it is not.

But it seems that there are many out there today who would attempt everything they can to convince you otherwise.

Illustration portraying bombs and a newspaper that shouts fake news

A collapse of trust

Ethan Zuckerman, a civic media expert at the University of Massachusetts, Amherst, says there has been an implosion of trust across the US.

"Americans don't trust big business. And we don't trust schools. We don't trust unions. We don't trust newspapers. You name anything, we don't trust it," he continues.

Zuckerman, recognized by Foreign Policy as one of its top global thinkers, argues the loss of trust may be directly tied to an erosion of faith in US leadership.

"In the 1960s, if you asked Americans whether they had confidence in the government to do the right thing all or most of the time, 77 percent of them said: 'Yes, I've got faith in the government,'" he says.

"By the time we get the 1980s and Reagan, we're down to around 25 percent of Americans who say they trust the government. By the time we get to Obama and then Trump, we're under 15 percent."

"So, if you don't trust the media and you don't trust the government, and you don't trust your work, and probably you don't trust your neighbors, who can you trust?" Zuckerman continues.

"And the rationale is: You trust persons on the internet who share the same points of view as you do."

Illustration portraying puppet masters leading the invasion of Iraq

The invasion of Iraq
Suzanne Schneider, who specializes in political theory and history at the Brooklyn Institute for Social Research, says it has encouraged a surge in conspiratorial thinking in the US as people, having turned their backs on traditional sources of information, look elsewhere for "truth".

"Conspiratorial thinking takes advantage of occasions when there are gaps in an official discourse, and it utilizes those defects as a chance to seed counter-narratives," she says.

"Conspiracy theories thrive when the sort of old ideological narratives start to come down, and they give some kind of consolation that someone is in charge of this mess."

Schneider uses the 2003 invasion of Iraq by the US as an example of how the government purposely altered reality to justify going to war. On February 5, 2003, the US briefed the United Nations with what it said was "solid evidence" of Iraq manufacturing and stockpiling weapons of mass devastation as a pretext for the war. That "evidence" was subsequently proved to have been manufactured.

"Certainly, a generation that lived through that struggle and some parts of the 'war on terror cannot look back and think that the government has been forthright with them," Schneider says.

Donald Trump's inauguration
"We like to think that facts lead to opinions, but in reality, ideas affect how we approach facts," explains Brian Schaffner, a professor of civic studies at Tufts University in the US. He specialized in the study of public opinion, political campaigns, and elections.

"When individuals already believe in something, presenting them a reality doesn't necessarily help because they want to look at that information through the prism of what they think."

The question of the audience size at Donald Trump's 2017 inauguration is a wonderful illustration of this point.

Though a photograph of the crowd at Trump's inauguration showed far fewer people than those photographed at Barack Obama's 2009 inauguration, Trump's Press Secretary Sean Spicer declared that Trump drew "the largest audience ever to witness an inauguration, period, both in person and around the globe".

Many journalists scoffed at Spicer's audacious distortion of the truth, but Senior Counselor to President Trump, Kellyanne Conway, jumped to his defense with the bizarre argument that the press secretary had only been deploying "alternative facts".

"Part of me is thinking, how many people are genuinely purchasing this right now?" Schaffner remembers, recalling his reaction to Spicer's inauguration comments at the time.

He decided to arrange a poll to examine whether anyone would believe Spicer's bogus allegations. His experiment would consist of displaying 1,388 American adults' photos of the two inaugurations, side by side, and asking the participants to say which photo included more people.

"This was a situation where we could show them genuine proof, like photographic evidence, and see if they would still tell us that, you know, something that's not true right before their eyes is true to them."

The conclusions of the survey were startling. People seemed willing to agree that two plus two equals five - with no torture necessary.

"Our trial suggested that 15 percent of American adults stated that they saw... in the one that had fewer people in it, they believed it's the one that had more people in it. And it was the one from Trump's inauguration," Schaffner continues.

How could it possibly be possible that people could truly make such simply refutable claims?

Todd May is a professor of philosophy from America's Clemson University and an expert in post-structuralism — how power systems impact our view of reality. He said he thinks it is because those individuals were so strongly involved in seeing a huge crowd that they were willing to swear they were confident the shot featured images that were not there.

"What we observe here is not merely a cynical type of lying, but true self-deception," May argues.

"If individuals are not prepared to accept their own eyes, but embrace a false ideology, then we're not going to be able to meet in reality."

And it is a major component of the issue.

Illustration illustrating two figures playing Scrabble with the terms truth and illusion

Neoliberal ideologues and 'the politics of deceptive populism'
Like those who sold the idea that Joe Biden's trip on the steps of Air Force One demonstrated that he was not suited to the job of leading America, many who profess to be purveyors of "truth" are scheming to distort reality for their political profit.

British author Peter Oborne, whose book, The Assault on Truth, investigates the manipulation of reality by politicians, says the twisting of truth was turbocharged by neoliberal ideologues who gained prominence in the US following the Vietnam War.

Oborne argues the neoliberal revolution "had a very harmful consequence in enfranchising politicians to invent new truths which aren't true – i.e., to convert reality to myth. This is crucial because it implies that truth doesn't become anything that is tied to something genuine. It becomes an expression of power."

"So, what you are doing, very intentionally, as a political tactic to win elections, is to create massive splits, deadly divisions in the long run, in society itself."

"The politics of deceptive populism is the best way of expressing it," Oborne argues.

"Manipulative populism is not about accomplishing actual things. It's about constructing false emotions built on anger and hatred."

The result: mistrust, uneasiness, suspicion, intolerance, rage-filled protests, and bloodshed.

President Donald Trump was eager to portray those heightened sentiments as proof that America was in decline. And he openly named individuals he felt were to blame.

"Trump tells people: 'Don't trust institutions of higher learning, don't trust colleges, don't trust professors, don't believe scientists,'" says civic studies professor Schaffner.

"And so, I believe he's given voice to something that has connected with certain people in a way that prior presidents simply were not ready to go there."

As if channeling the German Nazi Party's propaganda leader Joseph Goebbels, who reportedly claimed that "If you say a falsehood frequently enough, it becomes the truth," Trump delivered more than 30,500 "false or misleading claims" throughout his term as President, according to the Washington Post newspaper.

The January 6 assault on the US Capitol
One of the most egregious of those falsehoods was Trump's proclamation that he won the 2020 presidential election "by a landslide" and that any reports to the contrary were proof that the election had been "stolen" from him.

"You don't yield when there's larceny involved," Trump stated on January 6, 2021, to a seething gathering of supporters. He then instructed the throng to march towards the US Capitol.

The gang stormed their way into the building, screaming for the vice president, Mike Pence, and the speaker of the House of Representatives, Nancy Pelosi, to be hauled into the street and publicly murdered. The insurrection left five individuals dead.

Though television images showed violent confrontations at Congress between Trump supporters and an overwhelmed police force, one member of Congress, Republican Andrew Clyde, subsequently claimed that the invasion of the Capitol had simply not occurred.

Clyde claimed TV images of the Trump fans hitting police officers "showed individuals in an orderly way keeping between the stanchions and ropes, taking movies and pictures".

"You know, if you didn't know the TV footage was a film from January the 6th, you would genuinely believe it was a regular tourist visit."

Is it even remotely possible that Clyde believed what he said?

In truth's parallel universe – the world of shape-shifting realities – a genuine answer to that question may never be found.

"We are in a world where the accounts of events, what politicians say, what others say, are completely detached now from a meaningful, underlying reality," Oborne says.

So, to many, it would seem, it doesn't matter that two plus two is not five. Or six. Or three. They are living, now, in a different reality altogether.

Illustration showing 2+2=5

Social media and an alternative reality
Increasingly, social media provides a vehicle for them to create those alternative realities.

"You can pull on any number of threads and very quickly find yourself in a world not only where someone is trying to sell you a conspiracy theory, but where they're pointing you to dozens of other sources that will confirm that same sort of narrative," says media scholar Zuckerman.

"And I think that reality, by which I mean a shared vision of the world and how it works, is now up for grabs," Zuckerman reflects.

"We now have a media system that is so diverse and also so divided that the struggles, politically, over the next 10 or 20 years, are not about the interpretation of facts, they're about what reality we live in."

Professor May says that people are now finding it easier to accept misleading narratives because they are being affected by political power structures that distort the facts much more readily than previously — by exploiting social media.

"Two plus two will never equal five," he adds. "You can't manufacture your truth, independent of that reality. On the other hand, you can interfere and urge people to believe certain things or behave in specific ways and that could influence them to alter the reality that they're living in."

Like a lady, I met at a pro-Trump event in Washington, DC, in January 2021, who was certain that Trump had been "robbed" of a genuine election victory. The divide between those who tell "the truth" and those who do not have grown so great, she claimed, that she no longer felt secure anywhere, not even in the once-comfortable suburbs of Pennsylvania, where she had lived for years.

"I dread life," she replied. "I was just chatting with a buddy of mine about learning how to hunt for deer with a bow and skinning it myself — we call it 'living off the grid.'"

Just in case things were even more terrible, in case she had to escape the gangs of roaming criminal immigrants — rapists and murderers – that Trump had so frequently claimed were rushing into America from Mexico and abroad.

Just in case society fragmented anymore, in if the riots she's seen

 on the news — prompted by the shooting of Black males by white cops – moved closer to her house.

"My aim, the goal of America, is to have a better life for the next generation to continue farther, and we're not going to," she said to me as she walked back to the pro-Trump gathering. She raised a placard aloft stating "Stop the Steal" and her voice was drowned in the clamor of others surrounding her: "USA! USA! USA!".

'When democracy dies
Many Americans like her offer a shared message that we are living in an increasingly scary environment. Life was better,

previously, they believe. They are sure of it; Donald Trump and others have told them so frequently, that it must be real.

The communications revolution that we are experiencing is changing our lives dramatically – and how it will transform future generations remains a matter of significant danger.

It appears that entire swathes of American society are volunteering to join the home controlled by Orwell's Big Brother. Unlike the character Winston Smith, they do not need to be forced to believe that two plus two equals five, but appear to do so voluntarily.

May thinks that, in the future, when we stop to connect according to the big tales that formerly held society together, we may be unable to share a "common reality".

"That may well be when democracy dies," according to Zuckerman. "If we have a sufficiently varied fact pattern that we can't agree on a single reality to attempt to collectively govern."

That is, certainly, a frightening concept for the survival of Western democracy.

George Orwell must be turning in his grave.

www.ingramcontent.com/pod-product-compliance
Lightning Source LLC
Chambersburg PA
CBHW050825250726
48653CB00006B/2434